GARFIELD
Classics
Volume Five

MY FIFTH CLASSIC COLLECTION
CONTAINS:

IN THE PINK

JUST GOOD FRIENDS

PLAYS IT AGAIN

First published by Ravette Publishing 2000

Printed and bound in Great Britain
for Ravette Publishing Limited,
Unit 3, Tristar Centre,
Star Road, Partridge Green,
West Sussex RH13 8RA
by Cox & Wyman Ltd, Reading, Berkshire

ISBN: 1 84161 022 4

Garfield
In The Pink

JIM DAVIS

© 1986 United Feature Syndicate, Inc.

© 1986 United Feature Syndicate, Inc.

3-17

© 1986 United Feature Syndicate, Inc.

3-18

© 1986 United Feature Syndicate, inc.

© 1986 United Feature Syndicate, Inc.

© 1986 United Feature Syndicate, Inc.

JIM DAVIS 7-29

GARFIELD'S
Believe it, or DON'T !

A CAT IN LUBBOCK, TEXAS GAVE BIRTH TO 57 KITTENS

© 1986 United Feature Syndicate, Inc.

WHEN ASKED HOW SHE FELT AFTER GIVING BIRTH TO QUINSEPTUPLETS, SHE SAID:

I'LL FEEL BETTER WHEN THEY START SLEEPING THROUGH THE NIGHT

Believe it, or DON'T !

JPM DAVIS 1-25

8-15 © 1986 United Feature Syndicate, Inc.

JiM DAViS

SOME PEOPLE LOSE WEIGHT

I JUST GIVE IT A TEMPORARY LEAVE OF ABSENCE

JIM DAVIS 12-4

© 1985 United Feature Syndicate, Inc.

© 1986 United Feature Syndicate, Inc.

JIM DAVIS 12-5

REMEMBER, GARFIELD, THERE IS NO GREATER FAILING THAN APATHY

© 1986 United Feature Syndicate, Inc.

SO WHAT?

JIM DAVIS 10-31

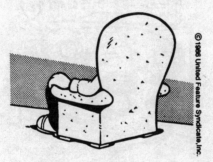

© 1986 United Feature Syndicate, Inc.

JIM DAVIS 10-6

© 1986 United Feature Syndicate, Inc.

JIM DAVIS 10-8

© 1986 United Feature Syndicate, Inc.

© 1986 United Feature Syndicate, Inc.

GARFIELD!

© 1986 United Feature Syndicate, Inc.

5-7

WHAT DID YOU DO TO MY FERN?!

I (BURP) PRUNED IT

JIM DAVIS

CRASH!

© 1986 United Feature Syndicate,Inc.

5-10

WHAT MADE YOU DO THAT?

MY SENSE OF AESTHETICS

JIM DAVIS

© 1986 United Feature Syndicate, Inc.

© 1985 United Feature Syndicate, Inc.

Garfield
Plays It Again

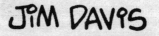

JIM DAVIS   ЯR

SQUEEZE

© 1986 United Feature Syndicate, Inc.

JIM DAVIS 12-16

SQUEEZE

ARRRGH!

© 1986 United Feature Syndicate, Inc.

© 1987 United Feature Syndicate, Inc.

STOP RIGHT THERE!

© 1987 United Feature Syndicate, Inc.

SOMETIMES THAT'S ALL A CAT UNDERSTANDS

© 1987 United Feature Syndicate, Inc.

© 1987 United Feature Syndicate, Inc.

© 1987 United Feature Syndicate, Inc.

GOINK
GOINK
GOINK

MUNCH
MUNCH
MUNCH

PTOOEY

© 1987 United Feature Syndicate, Inc.

© 1987 United Feature Syndicate, Inc.

SEE ANYTHING YOU LIKE?

JIM DAVIS 4-14

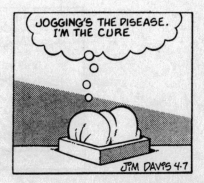

OTHER GARFIELD BOOKS AVAILABLE

Pocket Books	Price	ISBN
Byte Me	£2.99	1 84161 009 7
Double Trouble	£2.99	1 84161 008 9
A Gift For You	£3.50	1 85304 190 4
The Gladiator	£2.99	1 85304 941 7
Great Impressions	£2.99	1 85304 191 2
Hangs On	£2.99	1 85304 784 8
Here We Go Again	£2.99	0 948456 10 8
In The Pink	£2.99	0 948456 67 1
In Training	£3.50	1 85304 785 6
The Irresistible	£2.99	1 85304 940 9
Le Magnifique!	£3.50	1 85304 243 9
Let's Party	£3.50	1 85304 906 9
Light Of My Life	£3.50	1 85304 353 2
On The Right Track	£2.99	1 85304 907 7
On Top Of The World	£2.99	1 85304 104 1
Pick Of The Bunch	£2.99	1 85304 258 7
The Reluctant Romeo	£2.99	1 85304 391 5
Says It With Flowers	£2.99	1 85304 316 8
Shove At First Sight	£3.50	1 85304 990 5
Strikes Again	£2.99	0 906710 62 6
To Eat, Or Not To Eat?	£2.99	1 85304 991 3
Wave Rebel	£3.50	1 85304 317 6
With Love From Me To You	£2.99	1 85304 392 3

(available Feb 2001)		
Gooooooal!	£3.50	1 84161 037 2
Bon Appetit	£3.50	1 84161 038 0

Theme Books @ £3.99 each	
Guide to Behaving Badly	1 85304 892 5
Guide to Being a Couch Potato	1 84161 039 9
Guide to Creatures Great and Small	1 85304 998 0
Guide to Friends	1 84161 040 2
Guide to Healthy Living	1 85304 972 7
Guide to Insults	1 85304 895 X
Guide to Pigging Out	1 85304 893 3
Guide to Romance	1 85304 894 1
Guide to The Seasons	1 85304 999 9
Guide to Successful Living	1 85304 973 5

Classics @ £4.99 each	**ISBN**
Volume One	1 85304 970 0
Volume Two	1 85304 971 9
Volume Three	1 85304 996 4
Volume Four	1 85304 997 2
Volume Six	1 84161 023 2

Miscellaneous

Garfield Address Book	£4.99 inc. VAT	1 85304 904 2
Garfield 21st Birthday Celebration Book	£9.99	1 85304 995 6

All Garfield books are available at your local bookshop or from the address below. Just tick the titles required and send the form with your payment to:-

BBCS, P O Box 941, Kingston upon Hull HU1 3YQ
24-hour telephone credit card line 01482 224626
Prices and availability are subject to change without notice.
Please enclose a cheque or postal order made payable to BBCS to the value of the cover price of the book and allow the following for postage and packing:

UK & BFPO:	£1.95 (weight up to 1kg)	3-day delivery
	£2.95 (weight over 1kg up to 20kg)	3-day delivery
	£4.95 (weight up to 20kg)	next day delivery

EU & Eire:	Surface Mail	£2.50 for first book & £1.50 for subsequent books
	Airmail	£4.00 for first book & £2.50 for subsequent books
USA:	Surface Mail	£4.50 for first book & £2.50 for subsequent books
	Airmail	£7.50 for first book & £3.50 for subsequent books
Rest of the World:	Surface Mail	£6.00 for first book & £3.50 for subsequent books
	Airmail	£10.00 for first book & £4.50 for subsequent books

Name ....

Address ....

....

....

Cards accepted: Visa, Mastercard, Switch, Delta, American Express

Expiry Date........................Signature ....